W9-BAR-815

GEORGE WASHINGTON

ENCYCLOPEDIA
of PRESIDENTS

George Washington

First President of the United States

By Zachary Kent

CHILDRENS PRESS ®

CHICAGO

George Washington's home at Mount Vernon, Virginia, as it looks today

Library of Congress Cataloging-in-Publication Data

Kent, Zachary.
　George Washington.

　(Encyclopedia of presidents)
　Includes index.
　Summary: Traces the life of the Virginia surveyor,
soldier, and plantation owner who became the first
president of the United States.
　1. Washington, George, 1732-1799—Juvenile
literature. 2. Presidents—United States—Biography—
Juvenile literature. 3. Generals—United States—
Biography—Juvenile literature. 4. United States.
Army—Biography—Juvenile literature. 5. United States
—History—Revolution, 1775-1783—Campaigns—Juvenile
literature. 6. United States—Politics and government—
1789-1797—Juvenile literature. [1. Washington,
George, 1732-1799. 2. Presidents] I. Title.
II. Series.
E312.66.K56　1986　973.4′1′0924 [B] [92]　　86-12896
ISBN 0-516-01381-5

Picture Acknowledgments

The Bettmann Archive—6, 27, 28 (top), 30, 33,
38, 51 (right), 61, 67, 71, 80 (right), 84, 89
(bottom)
Howard Frank Collection—75 (left)
Historical Pictures Service—12, 13 (4 bottom
photos), 16, 17, 18, 20, 21, 22, 26, 28 (bottom),
29 (top left and top right), 43, 44, 55, 57
(2 photos), 58, 60 (top left, center, bottom left,
bottom right), 63, 64, 65, 76, 78, 79, 80 (left),
81, 85, 89 (top)
Library of Congress—14, 24, 25, 31 (bottom
right), 34, 53, 70, 74, 82
Mount Vernon Ladies Association—29 (center,
bottom left, bottom right), 88 (2 photos)
National Archives—87
© Nawrocki Stock Photo—42, 54, 73
North Wind Picture Archives—8, 10, 13 (top),
31 (top left, top right, bottom left), 32, 37, 41,
46, 49, 50, 51 (left), 60 (top right), 66, 69, 75
(right)
H. Armstrong Roberts—68
Roloc Color Slides—4, 5, 9
U.S. Bureau of Printing and Engraving—2, 31
(top center)

Cover design and illustration by
Steven Gaston Dobson

Mount Rushmore National Monument in the Black Hills of South Dakota. In this gigantic mountainside sculpture, George Washington's face is sixty feet high from chin to forehead. The other presidents on the mountain are Thomas Jefferson, Theodore Roosevelt, and Abraham Lincoln.

Table of Contents

Chapter 1

Starting a Journey to Greatness

Thirteen booming cannon shook the people of New York City awake on April 30, 1789. One cracking shot after another thundered through the dawn. Those who heard the noisy salute understood its meaning and greeted it with joy. On that day George Washington was to be sworn in as the first president of the United States.

While church bells rang and excited New Yorkers gathered in front of his Cherry Street house, Washington prepared for the most important event of his life. The fifty-seven-year-old former commander of the Continental army powdered his hair and dressed in a brown suit of Connecticut broadcloth. He pulled on white silk stockings and shoes with silver buckles. Finally he put on his dress sword in its shining steel scabbard.

The tall Virginian fully realized the heavy responsibility before him. Most citizens agreed that only he had the strength and skill to lead the country through its early years. With only the laws of the brand-new Constitution to guide him, Washington worried, "I should consider myself as entering upon an unexplored field [surrounded] on every side with clouds and darkness."

Opposite page: Washington's inauguration, April 30, 1789   7

Washington's neighbors greeting him on the way to his inauguration

While journeying northward for his inauguration, Washington admitted he felt "more anxious and painful sensations than I have words to express." Though cheering crowds celebrated his progress all along the route from his estate in Virginia, the general was not entirely at ease.

Just after noon on April 30 several congressmen arrived at Cherry Street to escort Washington to Federal Hall, the temporary seat of government. America was about to begin its great experiment in democracy. A throng of people glimpsed the general climbing into a grand carriage. They watched as four fine horses drew the coach away. The crowds pressed close, while bands blared patriotic tunes. Outside Federal Hall militiamen snapped to attention. Washington stepped from the carriage and walked inside the columned building and up a flight of stairs.

Washington takes the oath of the presidency, swearing to "preserve, protect, and defend the Constitution."

John Adams, soon to be vice-president, met him and announced, "Sir, the Senate and the House of Representatives are ready to attend you to take the oath required by the Constitution."

"I am ready to proceed," answered Washington.

Adams led the way onto a small balcony that overlooked Wall and Broad streets. As Washington approached the railing, a tremendous welcome burst upon his ears. The shouting people jammed the streets below. They swarmed on the neighboring rooftops and leaned from every window ledge. Washington bowed several times and touched his hand to his heart in a show of thanks. Soon Robert R. Livingston, the chancellor of New York, stepped forward and faced Washington. Standing between the two men, Samuel A. Otis, secretary of the Senate, held a Bible on a red velvet cushion.

Throngs of Americans celebrated the inauguration of their first president.

Washington placed his right hand upon the Bible before Livingston began: "Do you solemnly swear that you will faithfully execute the office of president of the United States and will, to the best of your ability, preserve, protect, and defend the Constitution of the United States?"

"I solemnly swear," replied Washington, repeating the oath word for word. "So help me God," he added at last, bending down to kiss the Bible.

Turning toward the crowd below Livingston shouted, "It is done. Long live George Washington, president of the United States!"

The people took up the cheering cry. It roared in waves through the streets as the American flag was raised on the Federal Hall rooftop. From ships in the harbor a great cannonade of guns joined in. The chiming of the city's church bells was almost drowned out by all the noise.

The country's first president bowed several times before reentering the Senate chamber. Duty required that he give an inaugural speech to the Congress. Shifting the papers in his hands, Washington seemed shaken with emotion. His voice remained so low that congressmen had to lean forward to hear.

"This great man," described Senator William Maclay, "was agitated and embarrassed more than ever he was by the leveled cannon or pointed musket. He trembled, and several times could scarce make out to read."

In his speech Washington asked that the American people be allowed to find "liberties and happiness" under a government determined by themselves. The power of his honest words moved many in the room to tears.

Following the ceremony Washington strode up Broadway, through the crowds and saluting militiamen, to attend a chapel service at Saint Paul's Church. In the evening he watched while all the city celebrated. Parades passed up and down the streets. Great bonfires blazed, and colorful fireworks displays filled the sky.

Touched by these signs of pride and affection, Washington still felt a terrific burden. To friends he would soon write, "I greatly fear that my countrymen will expect too much from me."

It was true that Americans put their faith in George Washington. But no other man could better fulfill their hopes and dreams. As a symbol of the American Revolution, Washington had led the nation over the rocky path to freedom. As president, they knew he would start the United States along on its journey to greatness.

Mount Vernon April 14.1789.

  I had the honor to receive your Official communication by the hand of Mr Secretary Thompson, about one o'clock this day. — Having concluded to obey the important & flattering call of my Country, and having been impressed with an idea of the expediency of my being with Congress at as early a period as possible; I propose to commence my journey on thursday morning which will be the day after tomorrow. —

  I have the honor to be
   with sentiments of esteem
   Sir
   Your most Obed.t Serv.t

    G.o Washington

Above: The Bible pages on which George Washington placed his right hand when he took the oath of office

Right: Inaugural buttons commemorating George Washington's presidency. (Front and back sides of the coins are shown.) The thirteen interlocking circles on the top coin represent the thirteen colonies. The March 4 date on the bottom coin is the day Congress was to have met to count votes and officially declare Washington president. But bad weather, travel difficulties, and lackadaisical congressmen held up the final count until April 14.

Opposite page: George Washington's letter to John Langdon, president pro tem of the Senate, in which he accepts the office of president

George Washington's birthplace on the bank of Pope's Creek
in Westmoreland County, Virginia

Chapter 2

A Kind of Destiny

George Washington's life began simply enough. On February 22, 1732, smoke curled from a farmhouse chimney near Pope's Creek in Westmoreland County, Virginia. Inside the plain brick house George Washington was born to Augustine Washington and his second wife, Mary Ball Washington. Over the next six years George's father carted the family from one tobacco farm to another. Finally they settled on a 260-acre farm called the Ferry Farm across the Rappahannock River from Fredericksburg, Virginia. As a youngster, George explored the neighboring hills on horseback. He swam and sailed in the clear waters of the Rappahannock. With a musket he stalked the woods that fringed the farm, hunting raccoon and deer. There is no truth to the story that one day he chopped down his father's cherry tree.

Whether Washington received much formal schooling is uncertain. Probably a tutor taught him basic reading, writing, and arithmetic. In one of his notebooks that survives today is a list of 110 "Rules of Civility and Decent Behaviour in Company and Conversation" that he copied

At fourteen, George had his bags packed and was ready to go to sea, but his mother persuaded him to stay home and help take care of Ferry Farm.

as a teenager. These rules seemed to guide many of his habits in later life. They included:

"Sleep not when others Speak, Sit not when others stand, Speak not when you Should hold your Peace, walk not when others Stop.

"Turn not your Back to others especially in Speaking.

"Wear not your Clothes, foul, unript or Dusty but see that they be Brush'd once every day at least.

"While you are talking, Point not with your Finger.

"Every Action done in Company ought to be with some Sign of respect to those that are Present."

When George was eleven years old, Augustine Washington died. For the next few years, while his mother raised his younger brothers and sisters, George helped run

George and Lord Fairfax riding at Belvoir

Ferry Farm. George's older half brother, Lawrence, often invited the boy to visit his plantation on the Potomac River. This estate, Mount Vernon, was named after Admiral Edward Vernon, with whom Lawrence had once served. George greatly admired his half brother and loved staying at Mount Vernon.

As Washington grew tall and handsome he often visited Belvoir, an estate located near Mount Vernon. There he attracted the attention of its owner, Lord Fairfax, perhaps the largest landholder in Virginia. On many bright afternoons the teenage George, by then an expert horseman, galloped off beside the old nobleman with yelping dogs on fox hunts. Attending dancing parties and teas at Belvoir, the shy young man soon acquired the polished manners of a gentleman.

Washington learned to survey land as a young man, and at seventeen he became the official surveyor of Culpepper County, Virginia. He kept up his interest in surveying all his life.

When Lord Fairfax sent a surveying party over the Blue Ridge Mountains to examine his land in the Shenandoah Valley, sixteen-year-old George hired on as an assistant. Stopping overnight at a backwoods cabin, Washington later wrote, he and the others "lighted into a room and I, not being as good a woodsman as the rest of my company, stripped myself very orderly and went in to bed, as they called it, when to my surprise, I found it to be nothing but a little straw matted together, without sheets or anything else." Before the month-long trip was over, Washington better understood the hardy ways of frontier life. He also returned to Mount Vernon with the valuable skills of a surveyor. He continued surveying land for other people and soon earned enough money to start buying property for himself.

Lawrence Washington's poor health interrupted George's surveying career in the fall of 1751. In an effort to cure his tuberculosis, Lawrence, with George as company, took an ocean voyage to the island of Barbados in the West Indies. It was the only time Washington ever traveled outside the boundaries of what would become the United States.

Unfortunately, the warm and sunny climate of Barbados helped Lawrence very little. Instead, George himself was stricken by disease. In his diary he revealed that he "Was strongly attacked with the small Pox: sent for Dr. Lanahan whose attendance was very constant till my recovery." Though Washington survived his sickness, it left his face forever marked by scars.

Within months of their visit to Barbados, Lawrence Washington died. In silent grief George determined to follow in his brother's footsteps and bring continued respect to the family name. Since Lawrence had served as adjutant general of Virginia, George applied for the position. Soon, at the still youthful age of twenty, he found himself a major in the colonial army.

Trouble was brewing in the Ohio River valley in 1753. From beyond the Allegheny Mountains trappers brought back alarming stories of new French forts and trading posts. British settlers complained of attacks by Indians who used guns provided by the French. In Virginia, businessmen of the Ohio Company demanded that their land and trading interests be protected.

Royal Lieutenant Governor Robert Dinwiddie searched for a messenger to warn the French to stay away from the

George Washington offers his services to Lieutenant Governor Robert Dinwiddie. Although Washington was young and inexperienced, Dinwiddie recognized him as a "person of distinction" and sent him on the risky mission to Fort LeBoeuf.

territory. When Washington heard the news he hurried to Virginia's colonial capital at Williamsburg. Striding into Dinwiddie's office he eagerly offered his services as messenger. At twenty-one the ambitious young officer stood over six foot, two inches tall with dark, reddish hair and gray-blue eyes. Though impressed by Washington's muscular size and noble bearing, the old Scotsman Dinwiddie still considered him to be a "raw laddie." But when no one else volunteered for the dangerous mission, Washington received the assignment.

The brown leaves of autumn crackled beneath their horses' hooves as Washington led his party of six frontiersmen into the wilderness. Through swollen creeks and over rocky mountains they journeyed five hundred miles. After

Washington and his guide Christopher Gist cross the icy waters of the Allegheny River.

some forty days, on December 11, 1753, Washington entered the wooden gates of Fort LeBoeuf, ten miles south of Lake Erie. Looking about, he observed cannon in the fort. Along the banks of nearby French Creek, his men counted more than two hundred birch and pine canoes. Clearly the French intended to stay.

Having delivered Dinwiddie's warning, the young major hurried back to Williamsburg to report this information. The return trip through the constant winter snow tested his endurance. When the horses grew too weak, Washington pushed ahead on foot. One day an Indian guide fired a musket at him before running away. Once he slipped from a raft and nearly drowned in the icy waters of the Allegheny River.

Washington's attack that started the French and Indian War in America also opened the Seven Years' War in Europe.

For his brave efforts, Washington was rewarded with a promotion to lieutenant colonel. When Governor Dinwiddie soon decided the French must be forced out, Washington recrossed the Allegheny Mountains leading a group of Virginia militiamen. In a skirmish that sparked the start of the French and Indian War, these inexperienced soldiers attacked a company of Frenchmen. "I heard the bullets whistle," Washington later exclaimed with innocence, "and, believe me, there is something charming in the sound."

Washington quickly established a fort, called Fort Necessity, to keep the enemy from the region. On July 3, 1754, French soldiers and Indian braves opened fire on the unfinished stockade. Since his men were greatly outnumbered and poorly trained, there was little Washington could do but surrender the fort.

In the spring of 1755 Major General Edward Braddock arrived in Virginia with a British army. Seeking knowledge of the frontier, Braddock accepted Washington as a volunteer on his staff. The Englishman intended to take his men over the mountains and attack the French stronghold at Fort Duquesne, where Pittsburgh, Pennsylvania stands today.

The thick forests of Pennsylvania were no place for a traditional army. Cutting a rough road through the trees, the redcoats slowly dragged useless baggage wagons and heavy cannon over the stumps and rocks. When Washington warned about Indian ambush methods, Braddock calmly replied, "These savages may be a formidable enemy to raw American militia, but upon the king's regular and disciplined troops they can make no impression."

On the afternoon of July 9, 1755, the French with their Indian allies surprised the long British column. Suddenly, screaming Indians appeared from behind every rock and tree. Clouds of arrows whizzed through the air amid a deafening burst of musket fire. Trapped on the narrow road, the British soldiers panicked. In terror men ran wildly about searching for escape. Officers on horseback, trying to restore order, presented perfect targets. In spite of the danger, Washington galloped back and forth shouting orders. Later he reported, "I had four bullets through my coat, and two horses shot under me, yet escaped unhurt, altho' death was levelling my companions on every side!"

Hundreds of soldiers fell dead. Many more wounded men lay moaning in pain on the forest road. At nightfall,

The defeat of General Braddock

after General Braddock himself received a fatal bullet
through the chest, Washington helped organize a hasty
retreat. The exhausted Virginian found no charm in the
sound of bullets now. This terrible British defeat
impressed on him an important lesson in warfare.

For the next three years Washington commanded border
defenses in Virginia. Another British expedition led by
General John Forbes in 1758 finally forced the French to
give up Fort Duquesne. With Virginia safe, Washington
resigned from the army at last. After years of gallant service the twenty-six-year-old returned home to find "more
happiness in retirement than I ever experienc'd amidst a
wide and bustling World."

The wedding of George Washington and Martha Dandridge Custis. Washington wore a blue velvet suit for the occasion.

One reason for Washington's happiness was his marriage on January 6, 1759, to Martha Dandridge Custis. A widow with two small children, the plump, short woman added a wealth of money and property to Washington's growing fortune. Cheery and sensible, she also taught her often rash husband the importance of calm thought and judgment.

While in the army, Washington had been elected to a seat in the Virginia House of Burgesses. Therefore, the bride and groom spent their first winter living at the Custis house in Williamsburg. As a gentleman, Washington enjoyed life in the Virginia capital. Always standing tall in a crowd, he cheered at local horse races. He

Washington at Mount Vernon with his family

strolled with his wife along the town's wide streets past fine houses with handsome gardens. In the evenings they went to the theater, played cards, or attended balls.

When the lawmaking session finished at the end of spring, Washington moved his family to Mount Vernon and settled down to farming. He would divide his time between Williamsburg and Mount Vernon during the next several years. But clearly he loved the country life best.

Rising at dawn, Washington rode horseback over his vast estate, supervising the tobacco planting. By 1765 he realized that constant plantings of tobacco ruined the land. Thereafter, he raised much more wheat and corn and enriched the soil with fertilizers.

Washington overseeing the farming at Mount Vernon

Throughout each day the Mount Vernon plantation bustled with activity and seemed like a self-sufficient town. Washington's many slaves tended gardens and raised pigs and cows. On the banks of the wide Potomac River they cast fishing nets. In open sheds blacksmiths shod horses and made tools, while coopers bent iron hoops for storage barrels. Some slaves tanned leather and hammered shoes at cobbling benches, while others sewed the home-spun clothes worn by everyone in the community. Content in the midst of these servants, his "family" as he called them, Washington happily observed carpenters add wings and a high roof to his house. In time Mount Vernon truly became a mansion. As gracious hosts, George and Martha often entertained friends and guests with pleasant conversation after a fine meal at their dining table.

George Washington pays his first visit to Martha Custis (above) and her children, Jacky (age 5) and Patsy (age 3). Although he had no children of his own, Washington cared for Jacky and Patsy and later adopted Jacky's two children, George and Eleanor ("Nelly"), shown in the family portrait below.

Mary Ball Washington
George's mother

Lawrence Washington
George's half-brother

Martha
George's wife

Martha Parke Custis
("Patsy")
Martha's daughter

John Parke Custis
("Jacky")
Martha's son

The tea-dumping incident in Boston Harbor was called the Boston Tea Party.

The years of peace Washington enjoyed at Mount Vernon were not fated to last forever. Following the French and Indian War, the British Parliament in London searched for ways to pay the army's expenses. One solution was to tax certain trade goods sent to the colonies. Forced to pay these taxes, Americans from Massachusetts to Georgia began grumbling about their rights. Many complained that King George III offered them no voice in Parliament. At town meetings angry colonists chanted "No taxation without representation!"

By 1769 Washington joined the protest by refusing to import taxable items from England. In 1773 he applauded the act of the Massachusetts men who, disguised as Indians, dumped a ship's cargo of tea into Boston Harbor rather than pay taxes on it. As the British enacted more disagreeable colonial laws, Washington warned that Americans must prepare to defend themselves.

Top row:
Samuel Adams,
John Adams,
John Jay
Bottom row:
John Dickinson,
Patrick Henry

In September 1774 delegates of the thirteen colonies gathered to discuss their complaints. At this First Continental Congress Washington attended as a representative of Virginia. At Carpenter's Hall in Philadelphia, Washington walked among the collected men and listened to their conversations. He met fiery little John Adams and his cousin Samuel Adams from Massachusetts. He observed John Jay, a lawyer from New York, and John Dickinson from Delaware. When asked to name the most impressive member of the Congress, the radical Patrick Henry replied, "If you speak of solid information and sound judgment, Colonel Washington is unquestionably the greatest man on that floor."

Washington hoped the British would listen to reason, but the crisis soon reached its peak. On April 19, 1775, in Lexington, Massachusetts, British soldiers confronted local militiamen. "Lay down your arms, you rebels," shouted a

The Battle of Lexington

redcoat officer, "or you are all dead men!" In answer Captain John Parker instructed his militia, "Don't fire unless fired upon. But if they want a war let it begin here." Suddenly shots rang out. When the smoke cleared eighteen colonists lay dead or wounded on the village green. The British soldiers pushed on to the town of Concord, searching for rebel supplies. During their return to Boston swarms of fast-arriving "minutemen" attacked them along the road, shooting from behind walls, fences, and farmhouses. The bloodshed of Lexington and Concord triggered the start of the American Revolution.

In May Washington attended the Second Continental Congress at the spired brick Philadelphia State House. Dressed in his blue and buff militia uniform, Washington silently revealed his willingness to fight. Delegate John Adams realized someone must lead the thousands of colo-

John Adams proposes George Washington as commander-in-chief of the Continental army.

nial militiamen then gathering outside Boston. Gazing across the room his eyes settled on the famous veteran of the French and Indian War. On June 15, 1775, the Congress resolved that "A General be appointed to command all the continental forces raised for the defense of American liberty." Seizing the moment, John Adams called out for the nomination of George Washington. By a unanimous vote, at the age of forty-three, George Washington the Virginia planter was elected commander-in-chief of the Continental army. Overwhelmed by his selection, Washington thanked the Congress. "I beg it may be remembered," he stated with embarrassment, "by every gentlemen in this room [that] I do not think myself equal to the command I am honored with." To his wife, Martha, he wrote, "As it has been a kind of destiny, that has thrown me upon this service, I shall hope that my undertaking it is designed to answer some good purpose."

Chapter 3

The Battles of the Revolution

Within a week General Washington galloped northward with a military escort. While journeying to Boston the general received news of a battle fought there. On Bunker Hill (actually Breed's Hill) just north of the city, rebel colonial soldiers held off the repeated attacks of British regulars, retreating only when they ran out of ammunition. Washington hurried forward, eager to see these brave men who fought so well.

Grizzled Yankee soldiers watched without interest as Washington trotted into their encampment on July 2, 1775. The army that encircled British-occupied Boston, Washington quickly realized, was not really an army at all. These militiamen often refused to obey the orders of the officers they elected. Undisciplined, they roamed the camp, dug trenches without method, and smelled in their filthy clothes. Though willing to fight, they were, Washington remarked, "generally speaking the most indifferent kind of people I ever saw . . . an exceedingly dirty and nasty people."

Opposite page: George Washington in battle gear

With uncommon energy the dignified general turned to the task before him. As he shaped the army Washington remarked, "In a little Time we shall work up these raw Materials into good Stuff." Throughout the summer and autumn months of 1775 the general drilled his men, strengthened his lines, and waited for supplies.

In January 1776 Henry Knox, a twenty-six-year-old bookseller who was the army's new chief of artillery, returned from an important mission. At Fort Ticonderoga in New York, Knox's men had loaded sixty cannon on ox-drawn sledges and dragged them through the freezing snow over rivers and mountains until they reached the colonists' lines. Excitedly Washington and his officers devised a plan to use these powerful weapons.

On the night of March 4, 1776, the dark figures of patriot troops scrambled onto the hills that lay to the south of the city. While thousands of laborers cracked the frosty earth with picks, 750 marksmen guarded the hills' approaches. With the light of dawn the British in Boston awoke to see Knox's cannon pointed down at them from Dorchester Heights. The stunned British General William Howe gazed at the finished entrenchments. "Those fellows have done more in one night," he exclaimed, "than I could have made my army do in three months!"

The British suddenly found themselves defenseless against bombardment. Within days Howe loaded his men onto ships and sailed out of the harbor. Soon joyful American soldiers and citizens packed the Boston streets. The siege was over at last. The Continental army had won a tremendous bloodless victory.

After hearing news of the Declaration of Independence, Americans tore down the statue of King George III on Bowling Green, New York. The statue, made of lead, was later melted down and molded into 42,088 bullets for the Continental army.

Washington correctly guessed the British fleet would sail for New York City. In April, long columns of his soldiers raised clouds of dust as they marched south to protect that important port. Immediately these hardy men set about constructing defenses on Manhattan Island and Long Island. When a dispatch rider arrived on July 6, 1776, with the news of a Declaration of Independence signed by Congress, the army stopped to celebrate. There would be no turning back now. Americans were determined to fight until they were free of England.

On July 12 lookouts spotted the stretched canvas sails of 150 ships sailing toward New York Bay. This British fleet commanded by Lord Richard Howe, the brother of General Howe, anchored off the coast of Staten Island. By the next day twenty thousand British soldiers and ten thousand German troops, called Hessians, had landed on the beaches. The Hessians were mercenary soldiers who fought for King George in exchange for money.

The American retreat at the Battle of Long Island

On August 21 British and Hessians began landing on Long Island. Washington's army now contained 23,000 men. Of the enemy, he anxiously wrote Congress, "We shall attempt to harass them as much as possible, which will be all that we can do."

At dawn on August 27 General John Sullivan's brigade of Pennsylvanians heard the piercing trumpets and booming kettledrums of a British band marching into battle. At the same time a hail of musket fire poured into their ranks. General Howe's dragoons and grenadiers had surprised Sullivan's men by circling behind them.

Attacked from three sides, the colonials retreated pell-mell for the security of Brooklyn Heights. By nightfall all seemed useless. Fifteen hundred Continentals had been captured. While the British regrouped, Washington saved the remains of his army by ferrying them in rowboats and barges to the safety of Manhattan. Once again he surprised the British by the quickness of his action.

Within days the British pressed the attack, landing on Manhattan at Kip's Bay, north of New York City. In anger Washington watched as his frightened militiamen dropped their guns and ran without a fight. When he could not stop them, he threw his hat to the ground. "Are these the men with whom I am to defend America?" he shouted. Unwilling to run himself, Washington was finally dragged from the field by aides to prevent his being killed or captured.

More disappointment followed during the next two months. As enlistments ended, many militiamen, tired of fighting, returned home. Hundreds of others deserted, skulking away from the army in the dark of night. The spirit among the troops fell so low that Washington complained they were "ready to fly from their own shadows."

Having lost New York City, Washington made a fateful decision. He agreed to split his command into four separate armies spread over many miles. On November 16, 1776, the general discovered the awful mistake of this plan. From his position at Fort Lee in New Jersey he heard the crackle of gunfire and saw billows of smoke rising from the heights of Manhattan across the Hudson River. Under heavy attack, the American garrison at Fort Washington had no way to save itself. In the evening Colonel Robert Magaw surrendered 2,800 men, as well as cannon and supplies. British Lieutenant Frederick Mackenzie walked over the battlefield. "Many of the Rebels who were killed," he observed, "were without shoes or Stockings . . . without any proper shirt or Waistcoat."

But Washington was determined never to quit. In early December he crossed his shrunken army over the Delaware River and sought the protection of the Pennsylvania woods. Surprisingly General Howe stopped his pursuit at the river's edge. With winter coming on Howe was content to return to the warm quarters of New York City with the bulk of his army. To control New Jersey, he left several strong Hessian outposts stretched across the state. Colonel Johann Rall, commander of the Trenton garrison, scoffed at the thought of the rebel soldiers hiding across the river. Experience had taught him they were "nothing but a lot of farmers." While the confident Germans played cards, drank fine wines, and prepared for the Christmas holiday, the farmer-general, George Washington, developed a daring plan. Remembering the surprise methods of the Indians, he decided to raid the Trenton garrison.

At sunset on December 25, 1776, 2,500 patriot troops assembled on the Pennsylvania side of the Delaware River at McConkey's Ferry. Along the water's edge the Marblehead fishermen of Colonel John Glover's Massachusetts regiment stood in dozens of boats, holding long poles. A stiff wind beat into the faces of the men. Officer John Fitzgerald reported, "It is fearfully cold and raw . . . a terrible night for the soldiers who have no shoes . . . but I have not heard a man complain." As the troops boarded the boats, Colonel Glover's men poled them the three hundred yards across the icy river. After a few hours General Washington sat in one of the boats and also crossed the Delaware.

The surprise attack
on the Hessians
at Trenton

After ten hours of hard work, the army was ready to
march the nine miles southward to Trenton. The snow
turned to freezing rain and back to snow again. The column stumbled forward in the darkness over the slippery,
rutted road. Washington rode along the line calling, "Press
on, men. Press on."

By dawn they were exhausted, but catching the enemy
completely unprepared, they poured into the village of
Trenton. The surprised Hessians, still groggy from their
Christmas celebrations, scurried half-dressed and in confusion through the streets. Hessian Colonel Rall tried to
rally his men, only to be knocked from his horse with two
fatal bullet wounds. In horror, German soldiers fled into
the woods, though most found themselves surrounded by
the rebels. In less than two hours the remains of the garrison, some nine hundred men, surrendered. Only four

Grateful ladies of Trenton staged a festive reception for Washington after his victory there.

Americans received wounds in the engagement. As news of the victory spread through the town, Continentals shouted with joy and threw their hats in the air. Nothing could have raised the spirits of the little army more than such a victory. Grasping one officer by the hand, Washington exclaimed, "This is a glorious day for our country." With one bold stroke he had given his men a sense of pride and hope.

Washington surprised the British again during the following week. Learning of the Trenton disaster, General Howe rushed several brigades to the town under the command of General Lord Cornwallis. On the afternoon of January 2, 1777, the redcoats found the rebels defending a weak line just south of Trenton. "I'll bag the fox in the morning," announced Cornwallis with confidence.

Washington's men charging ahead at the Battle of Princeton

That night while British sentries watched the lights of the distant rebel campfires, certain the Americans slept, Washington secretly hurried his men into formation. Instead of waiting to be captured, they marched all night and struck the British garrison at Princeton, New Jersey, the next morning. Shocked to find the Continentals where they least expected them, the redcoats fell back in fright. Charging on horseback into the face of the enemy, Washington excitedly called behind him, "Bring up the troops. . . . The day is ours!"

Defeated at Princeton and unable to catch the rebels, the British returned to New York City. With the double victories of Trenton and Princeton, people throughout the colonies recognized the greatness of George Washington. Proclaimed the *Pennsylvania Journal:* "Washington retreats like a General and acts like a hero."

43

The Marquis de Lafayette wounded at Brandywine Creek

The Continental army during the dismal year of 1777 needed just such a leader. After a harsh winter spent in the woods of Jockey Hollow near Morristown, New Jersey, Washington once again put his hardened soldiers on the road. In July spies reported General Howe had sailed his army from New York City and planned to land them in Pennsylvania. Washington shifted his troops into that state to protect the city of Philadelphia.

Among the new officers on Washington's staff that summer was the Marquis de Lafayette, recently arrived from France. Impressed with the ideals and energy of the twenty-year-old nobleman, the Congress commissioned him a major general. A great bond of friendship grew between gray-haired Washington and the younger man. At Brandywine Creek on September 11, 1777, a bullet cut through Lafayette's leg during his first fight with the enemy. As surgeons tended the wound Washington stood at their shoulders. "Treat him as if he were my son," he insisted, "for I love him as if he were."

During the Battle of Brandywine, General Howe's troops circled around the Americans, just as they had done on Long Island. Sweeping the colonials aside, the redcoats advanced into Philadelphia. Horse hooves clattered on the brick streets of the city, as congressmen hurried away to avoid capture.

On October 3, 1777, General Washington tried to dislodge the British at Germantown, a Philadelphia suburb. Confused by a heavy fog, patriot soldiers ran in all directions and even fired on each other. In panic, they soon fled the battlefield, leaving Washington to wonder why "the most flattering hopes of victory" had "turned into a rout." While the British sat and ate around cozy fires in the houses of Philadelphia, Washington led the remains of his army to a hilly winter camp called Valley Forge eighteen miles to the northwest.

Dr. Albigence Waldo described the first cruel days that winter: "Poor food—hard lodging—cold weather—fatigue—nasty clothes—nasty cookery. . . smoke and cold, hunger and filthiness. A pox on my bad luck." The men set out at once to build shelters. Axmen chopped down trees, cut them into lengths, and notched them to fit together. Soldiers hauled mud from the nearest stream to chink the cracks between the logs.

In a few weeks a thousand cabins covered the hills, each measuring fourteen by sixteen feet. Crudely constructed, their thinly thatched roofs leaked and dirt floors remained cold and dank. As many as twelve men in every cabin huddled before smoky fireplaces while icy breezes blew in beneath the doors.

A bedraggled sentry at Valley Forge. By the end of the winter, one-fourth of the men who camped at Valley Forge had died.

In December the food supply of the army ran out. The men chanted "No meat! No meat!" and made meals of "fire cake," a tasteless paste of flour and water baked over hot stones. Washington sent foraging parties to scour the countryside for food, but the wagons often returned empty.

While the men starved without food, they also froze for want of clothes. Dr. Waldo recorded a picture of the typical soldier. "His bare feet are seen through his worn-out shoes, his legs nearly naked from the tattered remains of an only pair of stockings, his breeches not sufficient to cover his nakedness, his shirt hanging in strings." On guard duty, some men stood with their feet in their hats to keep their toes from freezing. General Lafayette sadly noticed that there were soldiers whose "feet and legs froze until they became black."

Prussian officer Friedrich von Steuben, though he spoke little English, trained the Continental troops during their winter at Valley Forge.

Lice infested the few clothes the Continentals wore and crawled in their dirty hair. Disease raged throughout camp. Before the winter was over more than 2,500 men would die of sickness. Washington walked through Valley Forge and knew only too well the condition of his soldiers. "I feel . . . for them," he wrote, "and from my soul pity those miseries which it is neither in my power to relieve or prevent."

Slowly the situation at Valley Forge improved. Colonial soldiers raided nearby counties and even New Jersey. In February wagons loaded with meats, vegetables, and grains began rolling into camp. The spirit of the army also rose with the arrival of a volunteer, General Friedrich Baron von Steuben. On the frozen parade grounds this German drillmaster taught the Continentals how to load a musket quickly. He showed them how to use a bayonet and how to march and move in ranks. Praising the soldiers when they performed well and raging at their mistakes, in less than a month von Steuben transformed the men of Valley Forge into professional fighters.

As the sun of spring thawed the earth, the colonials regained their confidence. At the end of April excited officers spread wonderful news throughout the camp. The government of France had recognized the independence of the United States and soon would join the war as an ally. "I believe no event," Washington remarked to Congress, "was ever received with more heartfelt joy."

Having survived their winter at Valley Forge, the soldiers were once again prepared for battle. The opportunity arrived in June of 1778. The new commander of the British forces, Sir Henry Clinton, ordered his twelve thousand men to abandon Philadelphia and march to New York City. Sweating in their red woolen uniforms and struggling under the weight of heavy backpacks, the British soldiers snaked through the New Jersey pine lands in a column that stretched a dozen miles. Following at a distance, Washington ordered half of his army to attack the column at Monmouth Courthouse. Washington gave command of the assault to General Charles Lee, though some officers suspected Lee of British sympathies.

Stripped to the waist under a broiling sun, the Americans shouted and charged the startled redcoats. But when General Lee's orders became muddled and careless the attack soon fell apart. Greatly angered to see soldiers streaming past him to the rear, Washington galloped forward until he found General Lee.

"Molly Pitcher" takes her husband's place after he was shot
at the Battle of Monmouth.

"What's the meaning of this?" he shouted. "Why all this confusion and retreat?" Lee stuttered some feeble excuses until Washington roared, "Whatever your opinions, sir, I expect my orders to be obeyed!"

On his tall white horse Washington raced back and forth among the troops, halting the retreat. Observed General Lafayette, "General Washington seemed to arrest fortune with one glance. . . . I . . . never beheld so superb a man."

Inspired by Washington and using General von Steuben's training, the patriot troops formed a strong defensive line. Throughout the 100-degree heat of the afternoon they fought off British counterattacks. On the battle line Mary Ludwig Hayes helped her husband fire his cannon and also fetched water for his thirsty comrades. Grateful Continentals would not soon forget the woman they nicknamed "Molly Pitcher."

"Light-Horse" Harry Lee leads a night attack on the British at Paulus Hook, New Jersey.

At the Battle of Monmouth it seemed that as many men collapsed from the heat as from wounds. But in the evening General Clinton ordered his redcoats to withdraw. The British retreated to New York City, which remained their military stronghold.

While he waited for the promised arrival of French assistance, Washington held his ragged force together as well as he could. To raise morale he allowed some of his generals to conduct raids on British outposts. In July of 1779 General Anthony Wayne charged in a bayonet attack with his Pennsylvanians over the ramparts of the British fort at Stony Point, New York. A month later, men under the command of General "Light-Horse" Harry Lee captured the entire British garrison at Paulus Hook, New Jersey, during another night assault.

General Benedict Arnold, America's first traitor, tells his wife that his treason has been discovered (left). Arnold escapes to the British warship *Vulture* (right).

These small successes were followed in 1780 by one misfortune after another. Winter headquarters back in Morristown, New Jersey, proved as cruel as Valley Forge had been. One soldier, Sergeant Joseph Martin, complained that for four days his only food was the bark he gnawed from birch twigs.

In May the British captured the city of Charleston, South Carolina, and began terrorizing the southern countryside. Worse yet, in September Washington discovered that one of his favorite generals was a traitor. General Benedict Arnold's plot to surrender the American fort at West Point, New York, shook Washington almost to tears. "Arnold is a traitor," he exclaimed to Lafayette. "Whom can we trust now?" Though quick action saved the fort, Arnold escaped into the British lines, avoiding punishment. His treason, however, made Benedict Arnold the most hated name in the nation.

A chance for American victory finally arrived during the summer of 1781. In July the Count de Rochambeau's army of finely uniformed French soldiers arrived in New York. These well-equipped French professionals found the American soldiers surprising. One officer, Baron von Closen, noted, "It is incredible that soldiers composed of men of every age, even of children of fifteen, of whites and blacks, almost naked, unpaid, and rather poorly fed, can march so well and stand fire so steadfastly."

Washington wanted to use the combined American and French armies in an attack on New York City. But his plans changed when he learned a large French fleet was sailing to Virginia. Lord Cornwallis's British force was at that moment encamped on the Virginia seacoast in the village of Yorktown. If Washington hurried he could catch the British in a trap. Using tricks and secrecy to confuse the enemy, Washington rushed his armies southward.

By September 28, after hard marching, Washington's 9,000 troops and Rochambeau's 7,800 Frenchmen reached the outskirts of Yorktown. Immediately the men began digging trenches in the sandy soil. French Admiral de Grasse promised to blockade Yorktown from the sea, while Washington's soldiers laid siege to the British camp. Unable to get help, it seemed General Cornwallis no longer had a chance. "We have got him handsomely in a pudding bag," exclaimed American general George Weedon.

On October 9 General Knox's artillerymen began firing their cannon into the British lines. Cowering near the beach, Hessian private Johann Doehla claimed the shelling "felt like the shocks of an earthquake." He saw "men

Lord Cornwallis surrenders to Washington after the Battle of Yorktown.

lying everywhere . . . whose heads, arms and legs had been shot off." Five days later, while the cannonballs continued to rain into Yorktown, French and American troops captured two important British forts.

Cornwallis now realized the hopelessness of his position. On the morning of October 17 a British officer waving a white handkerchief stepped toward the American lines. Soon his message was delivered into Washington's hands. Cornwallis wished to "settle terms for . . . surrender." Two days later, Cornwallis's soldiers marched out of Yorktown. Passing between two long rows of French and American troops, they threw their weapons into piles.

The loss of Yorktown dashed all British hopes of keeping the thirteen colonies. While Benjamin Franklin, John Adams, and John Jay met British diplomats in Paris to negotiate a peace treaty, Washington returned with his army to the camps near New York City.

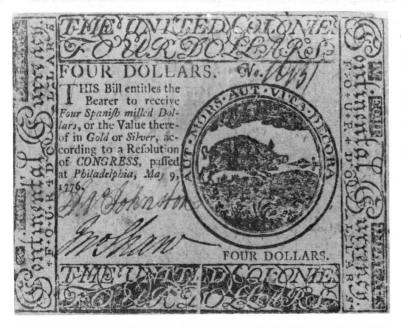

The Continental Congress issued about $240 million worth of continental currency (left). But few merchants would accept the bills. The $4 bill (top) shows a boar rushing at the hunter's spear and a Latin motto meaning "Either death or an honorable life." This meant that the colonists would rather die than be enslaved. The $5 bill (bottom) shows a bleeding hand trying to grasp a thorny bush. The bush is America, armed for a fight; the hand is England, trying to crush America. The motto means "Sustain or abstain"—put up with me or leave me alone. The Spanish milled dollar or "piece of eight" (below) was commonly-used money in the colonies. It was cut into eight pieces, or "bits," to make change. That is why a quarter today is sometimes called "two bits."

During long and idle days these soldiers sat around their fires and worried about their futures. Congress paid them with valueless paper money called "continentals" until the phrase "not worth a continental" became commonplace.

Washington indignantly refuses the suggestion that he make himself king of America.

With peace, the soldiers realized they would have to return home without money or jobs. Many blamed Congress for not taking care of them. One officer, Colonel Lewis Nicola, wrote Washington a letter in May 1782 urging the commander-in-chief to seize control of the government and make himself a king.

In astonishment Washington replied, "No occurrence in the course of the war has given me more painful sensations. . . . You could not have found a person to whom your schemes are more disagreeable."

In the next year, when angry officers threatened to overthrow the government themselves, Washington showed his great patriotism again. On March 15, 1783, in

Newburgh, New York, he called a meeting of the hostile officers. Standing alone before them he begged that they not take the law into their own hands and throw the nation into chaos. Unmoved by Washington's pleas, the soldiers continued to glare at him. Searching in despair for something more to say, Washington pulled a congressman's letter from his pocket. It promised better treatment in the future. Slowly he read a few lines aloud and then stopped to put on a pair of eyeglasses. "Gentlemen, you must pardon me," he apologized. "I have grown gray in your service, and now I am going blind."

Stunned by this quiet remark, which told so much of Washington's personal sacrifice throughout the war, the hardened men in the room suddenly found themselves blinking back tears. In an instant the general had reawakened in them their honest love for their country.

In the fall of 1783 Washington departed from the army after eight long years of service. The war was over. The last British soldiers had sailed from New York City on November 25, just as the American army marched in to take control of the city. Eager to return home at last, Washington held a farewell dinner at the Fraunces Tavern on December 4. Each of his trusted officers wept as he embraced them and said good-bye. "With a heart full of love and gratitude, I now take leave of you," he told them. By evening he was galloping southward to resign his commission as commander-in-chief to Congress. Though no man could have achieved all that Washington had done in the army, no man more cheerfully gave up his power when his duty was done.

Above: Washington's emotional farewell to his officers
Below: Washington resigning his commission as commander-in-chief

George Washington strolling through his Mount Vernon estate

Chapter 4

Walking Untrodden Ground

His greatness recognized throughout the world, at the age of fifty-one George Washington resumed his peaceful life at Mount Vernon. "At length, my dear Marquis," he wrote to Lafayette, "I am become a private citizen on the banks of the Potomac. . . . Free from the bustles of a camp and the busy scenes of public life." Turning his attentions to his long-neglected estate, Washington installed new wallpaper and bookshelves inside the house. Outside, he designed a greenhouse and laid out lovely walks and gardens. Every day he visited the five separate farms he owned around Mount Vernon and oversaw the activities of his more than two hundred slaves. Raising horses and hunting dogs gave Washington particular enjoyment.

Always a kind host, the retired general entertained every curious traveler who walked up his drive. Mount Vernon, remarked Washington, could be "compared to a well-resorted tavern, as scarcely any strangers who are going from North to South, or from South to North, do not spend a day or two at it." To a former staff officer, David Humphreys, he wrote, "My manner of living is plain. A glass of wine and a bit of mutton are always ready, and

1757
Age 25

1772
Age 40

1787
Age 55

1790
Age 58

1796
Age 64

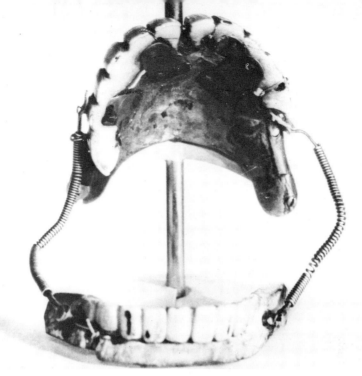

Above: George Washington's false teeth, made of hippopotamus tusk
Opposite page: Various portraits of George Washington

such as will be content to partake of them are welcome."
So many visitors stayed under his roof that it was not until
June of 1785—a year and a half after retiring—that he
could remark in his diary: "Dined only with Mrs.
Washington, which I believe is the first instance of it since
my retirement from public life."

Among the guests at Mount Vernon were artists who
wished to paint portraits of the famous general. With his
hair brushed back and tied in a queue, Washington sat
patiently while these men drew his straight nose, his clear
eyes, and other handsome features on canvas. During his
life Washington had lost most of his teeth, so while posing
he often kept his lips pressed together. This gave him a
stern appearance. It was the practice in those days to pull
aching teeth rather than repair them, so eventually he
wore false teeth made from hippopotamus tusk.

As the years passed, Washington watched the progress of the new nation with growing concern. Operating under its loose Articles of Confederation, the Congress possessed little power over the thirteen separate states. Confessed Washington, "I predict the worst consequences from a half-starved, limping government, always moving upon crutches and tottering at every step." The country needed stronger laws to hold the states together.

Other important businessmen, landowners, and politicians agreed with Washington's views. They called for a convention to revise the Articles of Confederation. Leaving the comforts of Mount Vernon behind, on May 25, 1787, Washington entered the Philadelphia State House as a Virginia delegate to the Constitutional Convention. With respect the other fifty-four delegates immediately elected Washington president of the convention. From his chair in the front of the room the general lent silent support during the important debates that followed.

Within days the delegates surprised even themselves by voting to scrap the Articles of Confederation. During the hot summer days that followed, these men decided to design a new government. In the ovenlike assembly room and later over tavern dinners, they argued about what form this government should take. Most saw merit in a plan submitted by delegate James Madison. It called for a strong federal government made up of legislative, executive, and judicial branches. Under this system laws could be made by a congress and carried out by a president, while the rights of the people were protected by federal courts. On September 17, 1787, Washington joined the

The signing of the U.S. Constitution on September 17, 1787

delegates, these "Founding Fathers," in signing the Constitution that outlined such a government.

Opinions varied sharply among citizens in the thirteen states, but slowly one state after another accepted and ratified the Constitution. Some did so with the understanding that certain changes, or amendments, would be made in the document. Others agreed to join the Union because they believed George Washington would be its first president. They felt that no other man but Washington could be trusted with such a powerful position.

In June of 1788 Washington stood on the porch of Mount Vernon and heard a booming of cannon from boats on the Potomac. People throughout the country were celebrating the adoption of the Constitution and its democratic form of government. The United States, a nation ruled by its people instead of by kings and nobles, would be something entirely new to the modern world.

WE the People of the States of New-Hampfhire, Maffachufetts, Rhode-Ifland and Providence Plantations, Connecticut, New-York, New-Jerfey, Pennfylvania, Delaware, Maryland, Virginia, North-Carolina, South-Carolina, and Georgia, do ordain, declare and eftablifh the following Conftitution for the Government of Ourfelves and our Pofterity.

ARTICLE I.

The ftile of this Government fhall be, "The United States of America."

II.

The Government fhall confift of fupreme legiflative, executive and judicial powers.

III.

The legiflative power fhall be vefted in a Congrefs, to confift of two feparate and diftinct bodies of men, a Houfe of Reprefentatives, and a Senate; ~~each of which fhall, in all cafes, have a negative on the other. The Legiflature fhall meet on the firft Monday in December in every year.~~

The Legislature shall meet at least once in every year, and that meeting shall be on the first Monday in December unless a different day shall be appointed by Law.

IV.

Sect. 1. The Members of the Houfe of Reprefentatives fhall be chofen every fecond year, by the people of the feveral States comprehended within this Union. The qualifications of the electors fhall be the fame, from time to time, as thofe of the electors in the feveral States, of the moft numerous branch of their own legiflatures.

Sect. 2. Every Member of the Houfe of Reprefentatives fhall be of the age of twenty-five years at leaft; fhall have been a citizen of the United States for at leaft ____ years before his election; and fhali be, at the time of his election, ____ of the State in which he fhall be chofen.

Sect. 3. The Houfe of Reprefentatives fhall, at its firft formation, and until the number of citizens and inhabitants fhall be taken in the manner herein after defcribed, confift of fixty-five Members, of whom three fhall be chofen in New-Hampfhire, eight in Maffachufetts, one in Rhode-Ifland and Providence Plantations, five in Connecticut, fix in New-York, four in New-Jerfey, eight in Pennfylvania, one in Delaware, fix in Maryland, ten in Virginia, five in North-Carolina, five in South-Carolina, and three in Georgia.

Sect. 4. As the proportions of numbers in the different States will alter from time to time; as fome of the States may hereafter be divided; as others may be enlarged by addition of territory; as two or more States may be united; as new States will be erected within the limits of the United States, the Legiflature fhall, in each of thefe cafes, regulate the number of reprefentatives by the number of inhabitants, according to the ____ rate of one for every forty thoufand. *Provided that every State fhall have at least One Representative*

note *&c.* Sect. 5. All bills for raifing or appropriating money, and for fixing the falaries of the officers of government, fhall originate in the Houfe of Reprefentatives, and fhall not be altered or amended by the Senate. No money fhall be drawn from the public Treafury, but in purfuance of appropriations that fhall *ftruck out* originate in the Houfe of Reprefentatives.

Sect. 6. The Houfe of Reprefentatives fhall have the fole power of impeachment. It fhall choofe its Speaker and other officers.

Sect. 7. Vacancies in the Houfe of Reprefentatives fhall be fupplied by writs of election from the executive authority of the State, in the reprefentation from which they fhall happen. V.

Above: The first page of the Constitution

Opposite page: Washington's working copy of an early version of the Constitution, on which he made notes.

Left: A march believed to have been written for George Washington's inauguration

Opposite page: Washington was touched by the greetings of those he met on the way to his inauguration. Always humble and sincere, Washington felt that the people put too much faith in him.

During the next months Washington witnessed with interest the birth of the federal government. People entitled to vote soon elected the men who would act on their behalf in Congress. Each state was allowed two senators, as well as a number of representatives based on population. Acting as an electoral college, according to the law, the members of the House of Representatives gathered in February 1789 to choose the new country's first president.

Though eager to help the country, Washington grew worried about his abilities as he waited to learn the results of the election. "My movements to the chair of government," he confessed to General Knox, will be like "those of a culprit who is going to . . . his execution." Finally a

messenger brought official word to Mount Vernon on
April 14, 1789. By unanimous vote, the electoral college
had chosen George Washington first president of the
United States.

Quickly Washington set off for the temporary capital in
New York City for his inauguration. At every town and
city during the journey north, cheering crowds pressed
around his carriage. At dinners they toasted him and lined
up to shake his hand. Honored with parades and speeches,

The crowds in front of Federal Hall cheered wildly as George Washington took the oath of office.

Washington saw the people were caught up in a democratic frenzy. Yet he remained concerned that they put too much faith in him.

On April 30, Washington took the oath of office at Federal Hall and swore to protect the people's precious liberties. In the days that followed he turned to the huge task before him. Nothing Washington would do as president had ever been done before. "I walk on untrodden ground," he commented. In its first year the federal government employed some 350 clerks and secretaries. Washington was expected to lead the entire nation without much more help than he used to farm his plantations.

Carefully the president chose men to advise him and head the government's departments. A former staff offi-

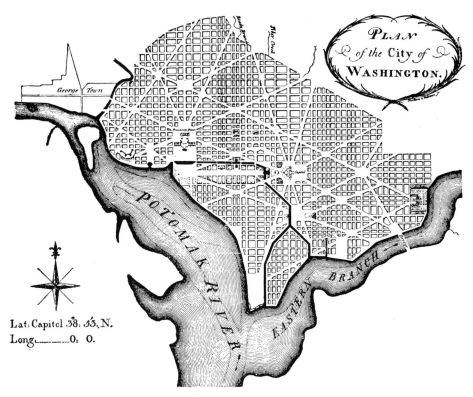

cer, thirty-four-year-old New Yorker Alexander Hamilton, joined the government as secretary of the treasury. With Washington's approval, Hamilton set about putting the United States on a sound financial footing. To pay the expenses of the government and erase national and state debts, Hamilton borrowed money from foreign countries and urged Congress to pass tax laws. To persuade southern congressmen to vote for his plans, Hamilton arranged for the permanent capital to be built in the South. Allowed to choose the site himself, President Washington picked ten square miles of swampy land across the Potomac River from Alexandria, Virginia. Here the federal city of Washington, in the District of Columbia, would slowly grow. But for the next ten years, until 1800, while streets were designed and buildings constructed, the government decided to make its home in Philadelphia.

Washington and his cabinet. Left to right: Washington, Secretary of War Henry Knox, Secretary of the Treasury Alexander Hamilton, Secretary of State Thomas Jefferson, Attorney General Edmund Randolph

For the last of his department heads Washington chose Thomas Jefferson, the writer of the Declaration of Independence. After returning home from service as minister to France, Jefferson agreed to become the secretary of state, representing Washington in foreign affairs. From the start Jefferson and Alexander Hamilton seldom got along. But Washington greatly respected both of these brilliant thinkers and carefully weighed each of their arguments before making any important decision.

With his department heads—his "cabinet" as they came to be called—in place, Washington turned to the duty of filling all the other federal jobs. From the village postmaster to the ambassador to Great Britain, no position escaped President Washington's interest. Every day he

The Ninth PILLAR erected !

" The Ratification of the Conventions of nine States, fhall be fufficient for the eftablifh-ment of this Conftitution, between the States fo ratifying the fame." *Art.* vii.

INCIPIENT MAGNI PROCEDERE MENSES.

Nine of the thirteen states had to ratify the Constitution before it could go into effect. In this 1788 cartoon, those first nine states are shown as pillars supporting the arches of government. Virginia and New York, the next two pillars, ratified soon after. Finally, in 1789 and 1790, North Carolina and Rhode Island gave their approval.

interviewed the many office seekers who came to see him. Vice-president John Adams admired Washington's industry and honesty in making all of his choices. "He seeks information from all quarters, and judges more independently than any man I ever saw."

After Congress passed the Judiciary Act, Washington appointed John Jay first chief justice of the United States. In long black robes Jay and the associate justices of the Supreme Court began deciding the nation's greatest legal questions.

Keeping their promise to the states, the members of Congress also passed ten amendments to the Constitution in 1789. Soon after, the two last hold-out states, North Carolina and Rhode Island, agreed to join the Union. Within two years the ten amendments, called the Bill of Rights, were ratified and added to the Constitution. They guaranteed Americans such basic liberties as freedom of speech, freedom of the press, and freedom of religion.

To foster a national identity among the states, President Washington traveled through New England in 1789. Visits to booming factories and seaports in Connecticut and Massachusetts pleased him as he saw the growing strength of the nation's businesses. In April 1791 Washington set out to tour the South as well. In the back country of North Carolina, South Carolina, and Georgia, innkeepers were amazed when the dusty carriage that rolled to a stop at their doors proved to contain the president of the United States.

As the population increased, adventurous settlers overflowed westward into the wilderness. One of the president's powers was to make treaties with the Indians with the "advice and consent" of the Senate. Expecting a quick response to a planned treaty with the Creek Indians, Washington one day entered the Senate for its advice and consent. Vice-president Adams read the treaty document aloud, but as Senator William Maclay noted, "Carriages were driving past, and such a noise!" The Senate doorkeeper closed the windows and the paper was read again. Then senators asked that additional papers be read. While Washington sternly waited, the senators next discussed the treaty and suggested that parts of it be postponed. Finally Washington jumped up and shouted, "This defeats every purpose of my coming here!" Though he returned and tried to be patient the next day, he finally stalked out of the room swearing he would never set foot inside again. Thereafter he communicated with the Congress by written messages only. For the next 120 years every American president followed his example.

Early treaties between Indian tribes and the United States were confirmed by a medal given to the chief of the tribe. The medal was eventually buried with the chief. The rare medal shown here is the token of a 1793 treaty.

GEORGE WASHINGTON
PRESIDENT 1793

Peaceful Indian chiefs sometimes traveled to Philadelphia to meet the tall, imposing man they came to call "the Great White Father." Many other people also met with the president. On Tuesday afternoons he opened his house to any respectable man who chose to visit. Describing one of these "levees" he wrote, "Gentlemen, often in great numbers, come and go, chat with each other, and act as they please. A porter shows them into the room. . . . At their first entrance, they salute me and I them, and as many as I can talk to I do."

The Washingtons entertaining guests

On Thursday afternoons Washington held formal dinners for government officials and their families. But he best enjoyed Martha Washington's tea parties on Friday evenings. Relaxed among the ladies in their handsome dresses and bonnets, the president chatted pleasantly while tea and cake were served.

These tea gatherings offered Washington an escape from the growing pressures of his office. With each passing day the differences between the followers of Alexander Hamilton and those of Thomas Jefferson became more and more intense. Their frictions gave rise to two political par-

Thomas Jefferson (left) and Alexander Hamilton (right) became bitter political enemies. After Jefferson became president, his vice-president, Aaron Burr, killed Hamilton in a duel over a personal insult.

ties in America. Hamilton's Federalists, most of them prosperous northern merchants, and Jefferson's Democratic-Republicans, primarily southern landowners, rarely agreed on the proper direction for the government. When Hamilton pushed a plan for a national bank that would benefit American business, Jefferson argued that it would be against the Constitution. Though a southerner, Washington desired to make the United States and its government stronger. Therefore, he refused to use his veto power to stop the bank bill from becoming law. "The evil genius of America," as Jefferson called Hamilton, had triumphed once again.

Chapter 5

A Second Call to Leadership

As his four years in office neared an end in 1793, Washington expected to retire to Mount Vernon. However, Federalists and Democratic-Republicans alike begged him to serve another term. As Jefferson told him, "North and South will hang together if they have you to hang on." Anxious to see the United States survive, Washington allowed the electoral college to choose him as president for a second term. He received another unanimous vote.

On March 4, 1793, in Philadelphia Washington took the oath of office again. At the age of sixty-one he faced four more years of national difficulties. The troubles began the following month when a young Frenchman known as Citizen Edmond Genêt stepped ashore at Charleston Harbor and rocked the country with his presence.

In 1789 a great revolution had swept through France. Common peasants and merchants rose up and threw King Louis XVI and other noblemen into prison. Waving flags of red, white, and blue, the people called for freedom from the hardships caused by the wealthy, royal class.

King George III
of Great Britain

Excited Americans compared the French Revolution with their own recent struggle with England. Throughout the United States they raised liberty poles, sang French marching songs, and toasted the new French republic. Thomas Jefferson and his supporters imagined modern democracy taking hold in that nation, too.

By 1793, however, ships were bringing less cheerful news from Europe. Starting with the beheading of King Louis, a Reign of Terror spread throughout the French countryside. Citizen courts condemned nobles. In Paris delighted mobs roamed the streets searching for more victims. In outrage, and to protect his own British kingdom, King George III soon declared war against France.

As Washington pondered what stand America should take, Citizen Genêt arrived as the new French ambassador.

One of many receptions given for Citizen Genêt throughout the country, as Americans rallied for the cause of the French Revolution

During his journey north to Philadelphia, Americans cheered his fiery speeches calling on them to join France in the war. In spite of public opinion Washington realized a war with Great Britain would ruin the United States. "If we are permitted to improve without interruption," he insisted, Americans had a chance to be ranked "among the happiest people on this globe." To protect the growing American economy Washington proclaimed strict neutrality. The United States would take no official side in the war between France and Great Britain but would instead balance itself between the two. This decision made Washington unpopular for a time in the United States. But as the nation continued to prosper people recognized the wisdom of neutrality.

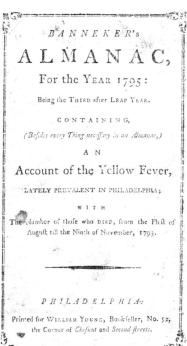

The almanac of Benjamin Banneker—inventor, astronomer, and mathematician—included tide tables, information on future eclipses, and data on victims of the 1793 yellow fever outbreak in Philadelphia. Banneker's almanac was the first scientific book published by a black American. He published six almanacs, from 1792 to 1797, in twenty-eight editions printed in various cities.

During the summer of 1793 an outbreak of yellow fever in Philadelphia threatened the government. President Washington led federal workers to Germantown, Pennsylvania, to escape the disease. Thousands of other refugees poured into the countryside. All business stopped. Funeral bells tolled for days in Philadelphia's churches. Before the disease had run its course, more than five thousand people lay dead.

The government faced other dangers in 1794. Warring Indians in the Northwest murdered the settlers who pushed onto their lands. To restore peace Washington at last sent an army under General Anthony Wayne into the territory. On August 20, 1794, these soldiers defeated the Miami Indians at the Battle of Fallen Timbers, near present-day Toledo, Ohio.

Closer to Philadelphia, President Washington dealt with another armed threat himself. Farmers in western Penn-

During Pennsylvania's Whiskey Rebellion, angry farmers persecuted officials who collected the whiskey tax.

sylvania often distilled their surplus corn crops into alcohol. When Congress passed a tax on whiskey, these angry men refused to pay it. In drunken bands they tramped the countryside, cursing the government and burning the barns of law-abiding citizens. Tax collectors scurried into hiding to keep from being beaten and covered with tar and feathers.

Alarmed by this open challenge of federal authority, Washington called for troops to put down the rebellion. Loyal militiamen from Pennsylvania, New Jersey, Maryland, and Virginia eagerly gathered to fight. A grand army of fifteen thousand men marched to the Allegheny Mountains. Washington rode to meet it. This staggering show of federal strength brought the Whiskey Rebellion to a rapid end. Frightened by Washington's force, the farmers rushed back to their homes and agreed to obey the law.

Mount Vernon, on the bank of the Potomac River, as seen in Washington's time. A visitor to Washington's estate wrote, "The house is most beautifully situated upon a high hill on the banks of the Potomac, and commands a noble prospect of water, of cliffs, of woods, and plantations."

Chapter 6

The Happy Life
of Mount Vernon

As his second term in office drew to a close, Washington examined the condition of the nation. Thomas Jefferson and Alexander Hamilton had both quit the cabinet by early 1795. As they continued to promote their separate ideas, their constant feuding troubled Washington. He believed the growth of political parties posed a danger to the government.

In every other respect, however, the young nation seemed to thrive. Tennessee joined the United States in 1796, further extending national boundaries. Laborers cut new roads through the forests, making trade among all the states easier. A new treaty with Great Britain gained protection for Yankee merchant ships. The American flag fluttered on hundreds of vessels carrying produce for sale in Europe. The thumping and whining of machinery could be heard in the mills and factories of New England. In the south, Eli Whitney's new invention, the cotton gin, made cotton crops extremely valuable.

Eli Whitney's cotton gin

Washington could be proud of his part in these accomplishments. By keeping the United States out of war and promoting its best interests he had guided it through its infancy. Many people hoped Washington would serve as president for life. But in September 1796 he published his Farewell Address in a Philadelphia newspaper. While calling for continued peace and justice in America, he announced his definite plan to retire at the end of his second term.

When the electoral college met that winter it chose John Adams to become second president of the United States and voted Thomas Jefferson the vice-presidency. On March 4, 1797, Washington attended the inauguration at the Philadelphia State House and observed the transfer of power. Following his example, no other president except Franklin Roosevelt was to serve more than two terms.

George Washington in his garden at Mount Vernon

Finally free of the burdens of public duty, Washington returned within days to the pleasures of Mount Vernon. Finding the house in need of repairs, he put men to work at once. Soon he cheerfully reported, "I have scarcely a room to put a friend into or set in myself without the music of hammers or the . . . smell of paint."

Every morning Washington rose with the sun and breakfasted at seven o'clock. "This over," he wrote, "I mount my horse and ride round my farms, which employs me until it is time to dress for dinner." After dinner (the midday meal) he chatted with friends and visitors, strolled about his gardens, had tea, and generally enjoyed himself. In the evenings he answered letters until bedtime.

In 1798 it seemed that the U.S. might be pulled into a war with France. In alarm President Adams called sixty-six-year-old Washington back into military service. For a few months Lieutenant General Washington organized the army until the crisis ended. Once more he returned to the happy life of Mount Vernon.

In December of 1799 as the cold weather began, Washington continued his daily rides about his farms. One day he returned home wet and chilled by stormy weather. When a sore throat developed he shrugged and said, "Let it go as it came." By the next morning, however, the former president was very sick indeed. An old friend and neighbor, Dr. James Craik, hurried to his bedside and two other doctors soon joined him. Following the medical practice of the day, they decided to "bleed" the patient by cutting his arm with a knife. The loss of blood further weakened Washington. On the afternoon of December 14, 1799, the old man whispered to his secretary, Tobias Lear, "I feel myself going. . . . You had better not take any more trouble about me; but let me go off quietly; I cannot last long." With Martha at his side, Washington died near midnight. Four days later his body was buried in the Mount Vernon family vault.

The news of Washington's death spread from city to town to backwoods settlement. All the nation mourned the passing of its greatest hero. As a soldier, politician, and patriot Washington had earned the love of America. In a memorial speech before Congress, Harry Lee rightfully praised Washington: "First in war, first in peace and first in the hearts of his countrymen, he was second to none."

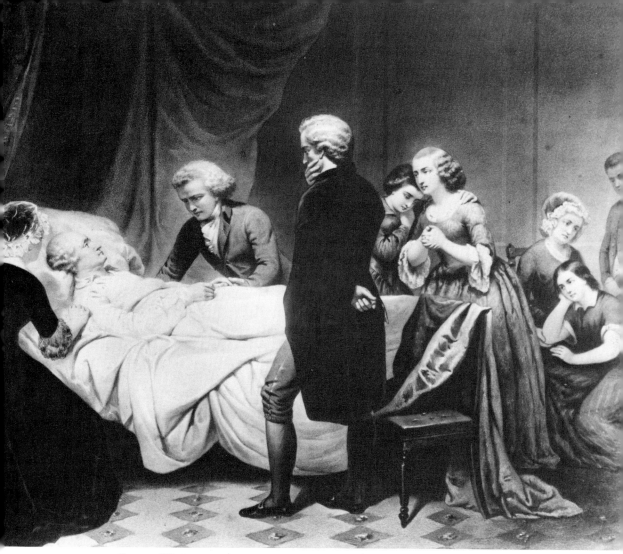

George Washington on his deathbed

To his wife, Washington willed most of his property, though he let his slaves go free. To the United States he left much greater gifts. He left it with a proud history and the chance for an even prouder future. Without children of his own, George Washington had instead adopted the entire nation. With love and affection he helped it grow until no other man could truly be called "the Father of His Country."

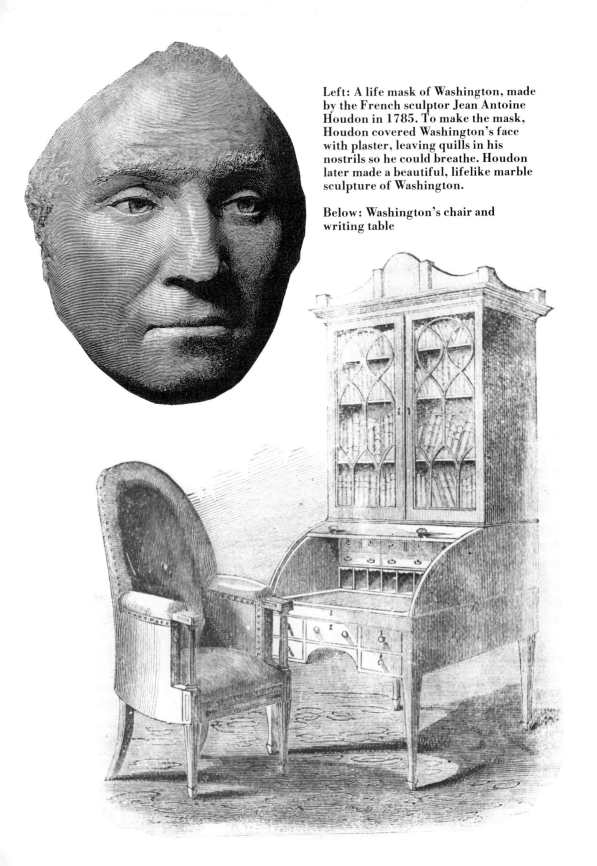

Left: A life mask of Washington, made by the French sculptor Jean Antoine Houdon in 1785. To make the mask, Houdon covered Washington's face with plaster, leaving quills in his nostrils so he could breathe. Houdon later made a beautiful, lifelike marble sculpture of Washington.

Below: Washington's chair and writing table

Above: Martha Washington's copy of *The Bull-Finch*, a collection of popular English songs. Below: The harpsichord that the Washingtons ordered from London in 1793

Chronology of American History

(Shaded area covers events in George Washington's lifetime.)

About A.D. 982—Eric the Red, born in Norway, reaches Greenland in one of the first European voyages to North America.

About 985—Eric the Red brings settlers from Iceland to Greenland.

About 1000—Leif Ericson (Eric the Red's son) leads what is thought to be the first European expedition to mainland North America; Leif probably lands in Canada.

1492—Christopher Columbus, hoping to find a sea route from Spain to the Far East, discovers the New World.

1497—John Cabot reaches Canada in the first English voyage to North America.

1513—Ponce de Léon explores Florida in search of the fabled Fountain of Youth.

1519-1521—Hernando Cortés of Spain conquers Mexico.

1534—French explorers led by Jacques Cartier enter the Gulf of St. Lawrence in Canada.

1540—Spanish explorer Francisco Coronado begins exploring the American Southwest, seeking the riches of the mythical Seven Cities of Cibola.

1565—St. Augustine, Florida, the first permanent European town in what is now the United States, is founded by the Spanish.

1607—Jamestown, Virginia, is founded, the first permanent English town in the present-day U.S.

1608—Frenchman Samuel de Champlain founds the village of Quebec, Canada.

1609—Henry Hudson explores the eastern coast of present-day U.S. for the Netherlands; the Dutch then claim parts of New York, New Jersey, Delaware, and Connecticut and name the area New Netherland.

1619—The English colonies' first shipment of black slaves arrives in Jamestown.

1620—English Pilgrims found Massachusetts' first permanent town at Plymouth.

1621—Massachusetts Pilgrims and Indians hold the famous first Thanksgiving feast in colonial America.

1623—Colonization of New Hampshire is begun by the English.

1624—Colonization of present-day New York State is begun by the Dutch at Fort Orange (Albany).

1625—The Dutch start building New Amsterdam (now New York City).

1630—The town of Boston, Massachusetts, is founded by the English Puritans.

1633—Colonization of Connecticut is begun by the English.

1634—Colonization of Maryland is begun by the English.

1636—Harvard, the colonies' first college, is founded in Massachusetts. Rhode Island colonization begins when Englishman Roger Williams founds Providence.

1638—Delaware colonization begins when Swedish people build Fort Christina at present-day Wilmington.

1640—Stephen Daye of Cambridge, Massachusetts prints *The Bay Psalm Book*, the first English-language book published in what is now the U.S.

1643—Swedish settlers begin colonizing Pennsylvania.

About 1650—North Carolina is colonized by Virginia settlers.

1660—New Jersey colonization is begun by the Dutch at present-day Jersey City.

1670—South Carolina colonization is begun by the English near Charleston.

1673—Jacques Marquette and Louis Jolliet explore the upper Mississippi River for France.

1682—Philadelphia, Pennsylvania, is settled. La Salle explores Mississippi River all the way to its mouth in Louisiana and claims the whole Mississippi Valley for France.

1693—College of William and Mary is founded in Williamsburg, Virginia.

1700—Colonial population is about 250,000.

1703—Benjamin Franklin is born in Boston.

1732—George Washington, first president of the U.S., is born in Westmoreland County, Virginia.

1733—James Oglethorpe founds Savannah, Georgia; Georgia is established as the thirteenth colony.

1735—John Adams, second president of the U.S., is born in Braintree, Massachusetts.

1737—William Byrd founds Richmond, Virginia.

1738—British troops are sent to Georgia over border dispute with Spain.

1739—Black insurrection takes place in South Carolina.

1740—English Parliament passes act allowing naturalization of immigrants to American colonies after seven-year residence.

1743—Thomas Jefferson, third president of the U.S., is born in Albemarle County, Virginia. Benjamin Franklin retires at age thirty-seven to devote himself to scientific inquiries and public service.

1744—King George's War begins; France joins war effort against England.

1745—During King George's War, France raids settlements in Maine and New York.

1747—Classes begin at Princeton College in New Jersey.

1748—The Treaty of Aix-la-Chapelle concludes King George's War.

1749—Parliament legally recognizes slavery in colonies and the inauguration of the plantation system in the South. George Washington becomes the surveyor for Culpepper County in Virginia.

1750—Thomas Walker passes through and names Cumberland Gap on his way toward Kentucky region. Colonial population is about 1,200,000.

1751—James Madison, fourth president of the U.S., is born in Port Conway, Virginia. English Parliament passes Currency Act, banning New England colonies from issuing paper money. George Washington travels to Barbados.

1752—Pennsylvania Hospital, the first general hospital in the colonies, is founded in Philadelphia. Benjamin Franklin uses a kite in a thunderstorm to demonstrate that lightning is a form of electricity.

1753—George Washington delivers command from Virginia Lieutenant Governor Dinwiddie that the French withdraw from the Ohio River Valley; French disregard the demand. Colonial population is about 1,328,000.

1754—French and Indian War begins (extends to Europe as the Seven Years' War). Washington surrenders at Fort Necessity.

1755—French and Indians ambush General Braddock. Washington becomes commander of Virginia troops.

1756—England declares war on France.

1758—James Monroe, fifth president of the U.S., is born in Westmoreland County, Virginia.

1759—Cherokee Indian war begins in southern colonies; hostilities extend to 1761. George Washington marries Martha Dandridge Custis.

1760—George III becomes king of England. Colonial population is about 1,600,000.

1762—England declares war on Spain.

1763—Treaty of Paris concludes the French and Indian War and the Seven Years' War. England gains Canada and most other French lands east of the Mississippi River.

1764—British pass the Sugar Act to gain tax money from the colonists. The issue of taxation without representation is first introduced in Boston. John Adams marries Abigail Smith.

1765—Stamp Act goes into effect in the colonies. Business virtually stops as almost all colonists refuse to use the stamps.

1766—British repeal the Stamp Act.

1767—John Quincy Adams, sixth president of the U.S. and son of second president John Adams, is born in Braintree, Massachusetts.

1769—Daniel Boone sights the Kentucky Territory.

1770—In the Boston Massacre, British soldiers kill five colonists and injure six. Townshend Acts are repealed, thus eliminating all duties on imports to the colonies except tea.

1771—Benjamin Franklin begins his autobiography, a work that he will never complete. The North Carolina assembly passes the "Bloody Act," which makes rioters guilty of treason.

1772—Samuel Adams rouses colonists to consider British threats to self-government. Thomas Jefferson marries Martha Wayles Skelton.

1773—English Parliament passes the Tea Act. Colonists dressed as Mohawk Indians board British tea ships and toss 342 casks of tea into the water in what becomes known as the Boston Tea Party.

1774—British close the port of Boston to punish the city for the Boston Tea Party. First Continental Congress convenes in Philadelphia.

1775—American Revolution begins with battles of Lexington and Concord, Massachusetts. Second Continental Congress opens in Philadelphia. George Washington becomes commander-in-chief of the Continental army.

1776—Declaration of Independence is adopted on July 4.

1777—Congress adopts the American flag with thirteen stars and thirteen stripes. John Adams is sent to France to negotiate peace treaty.

1778—France declares war against Great Britain and becomes U.S. ally.

1779—British surrender to Americans at Vincennes. Thomas Jefferson is elected governor of Virginia. James Madison is elected to the Continental Congress.

1780—Benedict Arnold, first American traitor, defects to the British.

1781—Articles of Confederation go into effect. Cornwallis surrenders to George Washington at Yorktown, ending the American Revolution.

1782—American commissioners, including John Adams, sign peace treaty with British in Paris. Thomas Jefferson's wife, Martha, dies.

1785—Congress adopts the dollar as the unit of currency. John Adams is made minister to Great Britain. Thomas Jefferson is appointed minister to France.

1786—Shays' Rebellion begins in Massachusetts.

1787—Constitutional Convention assembles in Philadelphia, with George Washington presiding; U.S. Constitution is adopted. Delaware, New Jersey, and Pennsylvania become states.

1788—Virginia, South Carolina, New York, Connecticut, New Hampshire, Maryland, and Massachusetts become states. U.S. Constitution is ratified. New York City is declared temporary U.S. capital.

1789—Presidential electors elect George Washington and John Adams as first president and vice-president. Thomas Jefferson is appointed secretary of state. North Carolina becomes a state. French Revolution begins.

1790—Supreme Court meets for the first time. Rhode Island becomes a state. First national census in the U.S. counts 3,929,214 persons.

1791—Vermont enters the Union. U.S. Bill of Rights, the first ten amendments to the Constitution, goes into effect. District of Columbia is established.

1792—Thomas Paine publishes *The Rights of Man*. Kentucky becomes a state. Two political parties are formed in the U.S., Federalist and Republican. Washington is elected to a second term, with Adams as vice-president.

1793—War between France and Britain begins; U.S. declares neutrality. Eli Whitney invents the cotton gin; cotton production and slave labor increase in the South.

1794—Eleventh Amendment to the Constitution is passed, limiting federal courts' power. "Whiskey Rebellion" in Pennsylvania protests federal whiskey tax. James Madison marries Dolley Payne Todd.

1795—George Washington signs the Jay Treaty with Great Britain. Treaty of San Lorenzo, between U.S. and Spain, settles Florida boundary and gives U.S. right to navigate the Mississippi.

1796—Tennessee enters the Union. Washington gives his Farewell Address, refusing a third presidential term. John Adams is elected president and Thomas Jefferson vice-president.

1797—Adams recommends defense measures against possible war with France. Napoleon Bonaparte and his army march against Austrians in Italy. U.S. population is about 4,900,000.

1798—Washington is named commander-in-chief of the U.S. army. Department of the Navy is created. Alien and Sedition Acts are passed. Napoleon's troops invade Egypt and Switzerland.

1799—George Washington dies at Mount Vernon. James Monroe is elected governor of Virginia. French Revolution ends. Napoleon becomes ruler of France.

1800—Thomas Jefferson and Aaron Burr tie for president. U.S. capital is moved from Philadelphia to Washington, D.C. The White House is built as presidents' home. Spain returns Louisiana to France.

1801—After thirty-six ballots, House of Representatives elects Thomas Jefferson president, making Burr vice-president. James Madison is named secretary of state.

1802—Congress abolishes excise taxes. U.S. Military Academy is founded at West Point, New York.

1803—Ohio enters the Union. Louisiana Purchase treaty is signed with France, greatly expanding U.S. territory.

1804—Twelfth Amendment to the Constitution rules that president and vice-president be elected separately. Alexander Hamilton is killed by Vice-President Aaron Burr in a duel. Orleans Territory is established. Napoleon crowns himself emperor of France.

1805—Thomas Jefferson begins his second term as president. Lewis and Clark expedition reaches the Pacific Ocean.

1806—Coinage of silver dollars is stopped; resumes in 1836.

1807—Aaron Burr is acquitted in treason trial. Embargo Act closes U.S. ports to trade.

1808—James Madison is elected president. Congress outlaws importing slaves from Africa.

1810—U.S. population is 7,240,000.

1811—General William Henry Harrison defeats Indians at Tippecanoe. James Monroe is named secretary of state.

1812—Louisiana becomes a state. U.S. declares war on Britain (War of 1812). James Madison is reelected president. Napoleon invades Russia.

1813—British forces take Fort Niagara and Buffalo, New York.

1814—Francis Scott Key writes "The Star-Spangled Banner." British troops burn much of Washington, D.C., including the White House. Treaty of Ghent ends War of 1812. James Monroe becomes secretary of war.

1815—Napoleon meets his final defeat at Battle of Waterloo.

1816—James Monroe is elected president. Indiana becomes a state.

1817—Mississippi becomes a state. Construction on Erie Canal begins.

1818—Illinois enters the Union. The present thirteen-stripe flag is adopted. Border between U.S. and Canada is agreed upon.

1819—Alabama becomes a state. U.S. purchases Florida from Spain. Thomas Jefferson establishes the University of Virginia.

1820—James Monroe is reelected. In the Missouri Compromise, Maine enters the Union as a free (non-slave) state.

1821—Missouri enters the Union as a slave state. Santa Fe Trail opens the American Southwest. Mexico declares independence from Spain. Napoleon Bonaparte dies.

1822—U.S. recognizes Mexico and Colombia. Liberia in Africa is founded as a home for freed slaves.

1823—Monroe Doctrine closes North and South America to colonizing or invasion by European powers.

1824—House of Representatives elects John Quincy Adams president when none of the four candidates wins a majority in national election. Mexico becomes a republic.

1825—Erie Canal is opened. U.S. population is 11,300,000.

1826—Thomas Jefferson and John Adams both die on July 4, the fiftieth anniversary of the Declaration of Independence.

1828—Andrew Jackson is elected president. Tariff of Abominations is passed by Congress, cutting imports.

1829—James Madison attends Virginia's constitutional convention. Slavery is abolished in Mexico.

1830—Indian Removal Act to resettle Indians west of the Mississippi is approved.

1831—James Monroe dies in New York City. Cyrus McCormick develops his reaper.

1832—Andrew Jackson, nominated by the new Democratic Party, is reelected president.

1833—Britain abolishes slavery in its colonies.

1835—Federal government becomes debt-free for the first time.

1836—Martin Van Buren becomes president. Texas wins independence from Mexico. Arkansas joins the Union. James Madison dies at Montpelier, Virginia.

1837—Michigan enters the Union. U.S. population is 15,900,000.

1840—William Henry Harrison is elected president.

1841—President Harrison dies one month after inauguration. Vice-President John Tyler succeeds him.

1844—James Knox Polk is elected president. Samuel Morse sends first telegraphic message.

1845—Texas and Florida become states. Potato famine in Ireland causes massive emigration from Ireland to U.S.

1846—Iowa enters the Union. War with Mexico begins.

1847—U.S. captures Mexico City.

1848—Zachary Taylor becomes president. Treaty of Guadalupe Hidalgo ends Mexico-U.S. war. Wisconsin becomes a state.

1850—President Taylor dies and Vice-President Millard Fillmore succeeds him. California enters the Union, breaking tie between slave and free states.

1852—Franklin Pierce is elected president.

1853—Gadsen Purchase transfers Mexican territory to U.S.

1854—"War for Bleeding Kansas" is fought between slave and free states.

1855—Czar Nicholas I of Russia dies, succeeded by Alexander II.

1856—James Buchanan is elected president. In Massacre of Potawatomi Creek, Kansas-slavers are murdered by free-staters.

1858—Minnesota enters the Union.

1859—Oregon becomes a state.

1860—Abraham Lincoln is elected president; South Carolina secedes from the Union in protest.

1861—Arkansas, Tennessee, North Carolina, and Virginia secede. Kansas enters the Union as a free state. Civil War begins.

1862—Union forces capture Fort Henry, Roanoke Island, Fort Donelson, Jacksonville, and New Orleans; Union armies are defeated at the battles of Bull Run and Fredericksburg.

1863—Lincoln issues Emancipation Proclamation: all slaves held in rebelling territories are declared free. West Virginia becomes a state.

1864—Abraham Lincoln is reelected. Nevada becomes a state.

1865—Lincoln is assassinated, succeeded by Andrew Johnson. U.S. Civil War ends on May 26. Thirteenth Amendment abolishes slavery.

1867—Nebraska becomes a state. U.S. buys Alaska from Russia for $7,200,000. Reconstruction Acts are passed.

1868—President Johnson is impeached for violating Tenure of Office Act, but is acquitted by Senate. Ulysses S. Grant is elected president. Fourteenth Amendment prohibits voting discrimination.

1870—Fifteenth Amendment gives blacks the right to vote.

1872—Grant is reelected over Horace Greeley. General Amnesty Act pardons ex-Confederates.

1876—Colorado enters the Union. "Custer's last stand": he and his men are massacred by Sioux Indians at Little Big Horn, Montana.

1877—Rutherford B. Hayes is elected president as all disputed votes are awarded to him.

1880—James A. Garfield is elected president.

1881—President Garfield is shot and killed, succeeded by Vice-President Chester A. Arthur.

1882—U.S. bans Chinese immigration for ten years.

1884—Grover Cleveland becomes president.

1886—Statue of Liberty is dedicated.

1888—Benjamin Harrison is elected president.

1889—North Dakota, South Dakota, Washington, and Montana become states.

1890—Idaho and Wyoming become states.

1892—Grover Cleveland is elected president.

1896—William McKinley is elected president. Utah becomes a state.

1898—U.S. declares war on Spain over Cuba.

1899—Philippines demand independence from U.S.

1900—McKinley is reelected. Boxer Rebellion against foreigners in China begins.

1901—McKinley is assassinated by anarchist; he is succeeded by Theodore Roosevelt.

1902—U.S. acquires perpetual control over Panama Canal.

1903—Alaskan frontier is settled.

1904—Russian-Japanese War breaks out. Theodore Roosevelt wins presidential election.

1905—Treaty of Portsmouth signed, ending Russian-Japanese War.

1906—U.S. troops occupy Cuba.

1907—President Roosevelt bars all Japanese immigration. Oklahoma enters the Union.

1908—William Howard Taft becomes president.

1909—NAACP is founded under W.E.B. DuBois

1910—China abolishes slavery.

1911—Chinese Revolution begins.

1912—Woodrow Wilson is elected president. Arizona and New Mexico become states.

1913—Federal income tax is introduced in U.S. through the Sixteenth Amendment.

1914—World War I begins.

1915—British liner *Lusitania* is sunk by German submarine.

1916—Wilson is reelected president.

1917—U.S. breaks diplomatic relations with Germany. Czar Nicholas of Russia abdicates as revolution begins. U.S. declares war on Austria-Hungary.

1918—Wilson proclaims "Fourteen Points" as war aims. On November 11, armistice is signed between Allies and Germany.

1919—Eighteenth Amendment prohibits sale and manufacture of intoxicating liquors. Wilson presides over first League of Nations; wins Nobel Peace Prize.

1920—Nineteenth Amendment (women's suffrage) is passed. Warren Harding is elected president.

1921—Adolf Hitler's stormtroopers begin to terrorize political opponents.

1922—Irish Free State is established. Soviet states form USSR. Benito Mussolini forms Fascist government in Italy.

1923—President Harding dies; he is succeeded by Vice-President Calvin Coolidge.

1924—Coolidge is elected president.

1925—Hitler reorganizes Nazi Party and publishes first volume of *Mein Kampf.*

1926—Fascist youth organizations founded in Germany and Italy. Republic of Lebanon proclaimed.

1927—Stalin becomes Soviet dictator. Economic conference in Geneva attended by fifty-two nations.

1928—Herbert Hoover is elected president. U.S. and many other nations sign Kellogg-Briand pacts to outlaw war.

1929—Stock prices in New York crash on "Black Thursday"; the Great Depression begins.

1930—Bank of U.S. and its many branches close (most significant bank failure of the year).

1931—Emigration from U.S. exceeds immigration for first time as Depression deepens.

1932—Franklin D. Roosevelt wins presidential election in a Democratic landslide.

1933—First concentration camps are erected in Germany. U.S. recognizes USSR and resumes trade. Twenty-First Amendment repeals prohibition.

1934—Severe dust storms hit Plains states. President Roosevelt passes U.S. Social Security Act.

1936—Roosevelt is reelected. Spanish Civil War begins. Hitler and Mussolini form Rome-Berlin Axis.

1937—Roosevelt signs Neutrality Act.

1938—Roosevelt sends appeal to Hitler and Mussolini to settle European problems amicably.

1939—Germany takes over Czechoslovakia and invades Poland, starting World War II.

1940—Roosevelt is reelected for a third term.

1941—Japan bombs Pearl Harbor, U.S. declares war on Japan. Germany and Italy declare war on U.S.; U.S. then declares war on them.

1942—Allies agree not to make separate peace treaties with the enemies. U.S. government transfers more than 100,000 Nisei (Japanese-Americans) from west coast to inland concentration camps.

1943—Allied bombings of Germany begin.

1944—Roosevelt is reelected for a fourth term. Allied forces invade Normandy on D-Day.

1945—President Roosevelt dies; he is succeeded by Harry S Truman. Mussolini is killed; Hitler commits suicide. Germany surrenders. U.S. drops atomic bomb on Hiroshima; Japan surrenders: end of World War II.

1946—U.N. General Assembly holds its first session in London. Peace conference of twenty-one nations is held in Paris.

1947—Peace treaties are signed in Paris. "Cold War" is in full swing.

1948—U.S. passes Marshall Plan Act, providing $17 billion in aid for Europe. U.S. recognizes new nation of Israel. India and Pakistan become free of British rule. Truman is elected president.

1949—Republic of Eire is proclaimed in Dublin. Russia blocks land route access from Western Germany to Berlin; airlift begins. U.S., France, and Britain agree to merge their zones of occupation in West Germany. Apartheid program begins in South Africa.

1950—Riots in Johannesburg, South Africa, against apartheid. North Korea invades South Korea. U.N. forces land in South Korea and recapture Seoul.

1951—Twenty-Second Amendment limits president to two terms.

1952—Dwight D. Eisenhower resigns as supreme commander in Europe and is elected president.

1953—Stalin dies; struggle for power in Russia follows. The Rosenbergs, first sentenced as spies in 1951, are executed.

1954—U.S. and Japan sign mutual defense agreement.

1955—Blacks in Montgomery, Alabama, boycott segregated bus lines.

1956—Eisenhower is reelected president. Soviet troops march into Hungary.

1957—U.S. agrees to withdraw ground forces from Japan. Russia launches first satellite, *Sputnik*.

1958—European Common Market comes into being. Alaska becomes the forty-ninth state. Fidel Castro begins war against Batista government in Cuba.

1959—Hawaii becomes fiftieth state. Castro becomes premier of Cuba. De Gaulle is proclaimed president of the Fifth Republic of France.

1960—Historic debates between Senator John F. Kennedy and Vice-President Richard Nixon are televised. Kennedy is elected president. Brezhnev becomes president of USSR.

1961—Berlin Wall is constructed. Kennedy and Khrushchev confer in Vienna. In Bay of Pigs incident, Cubans trained by CIA attempt to overthrow Castro.

1962—U.S. military council is established in South Vietnam.

1963—Riots and beatings by police and whites mark civil rights demonstrations in Birmingham, Alabama; 30,000 troops are called out, Martin Luther King, Jr., is arrested. Freedom marchers descend on Washington, D.C., to demonstrate. President Kennedy is assassinated; Vice-President Lyndon B. Johnson is sworn in as president.

1964—U.S. aircraft bomb North Vietnam. Johnson is elected president.

1965—U.S. combat troops arrive in South Vietnam.

1966—International Days of Protest against U.S. policy in Vietnam. National Guard quells race riots in Chicago.

1967—Six-Day War between Israel and Arab nations.

1968—Martin Luther King, Jr., is assassinated in Memphis, Tennessee. Senator Robert Kennedy is assassinated in Los Angeles. Riots and police brutality take place at Democratic National Convention in Chicago. Richard Nixon is elected president. Czechoslovakia is invaded by Soviet and Warsaw Pact troops.

1969—Hundreds of thousands of people in several U.S. cities demonstrate against Vietnam War.

1970—Four Vietnam War protesters are killed by National Guardsmen at Kent State University in Ohio.

1971—Twenty-Sixth Amendment allows eighteen-year-olds to vote.

1972—Nixon visits Communist China; is reelected president in near-record landslide. Watergate affair begins when five men are arrested in the Watergate hotel complex in Washington, D.C. Nixon announces resignations of aides Haldeman, Ehrlichman, and Dean and Attorney General Kleindienst as a result of Watergate-related charges.

1973—Vice-President Spiro Agnew resigns; Gerald Ford is named vice-president. Vietnam peace treaty is formally approved after nineteen months of negotiations.

1974—As a result of Watergate cover-up, impeachment is considered; Nixon resigns and Ford becomes president. Ford pardons Nixon and grants limited amnesty to Vietnam War draft evaders and military deserters.

1975—U.S. civilians are evacuated from Saigon, South Vietnam, as Communist forces complete takeover of South Vietnam.

1976—U.S. celebrates its Bicentennial. James Earl Carter becomes president.

1977—Carter pardons most Vietnam draft evaders, numbering some 10,000.

1980—Ronald Reagan is elected president.

1981—President Reagan is shot in the chest in assassination attempt. Sandra Day O'Connor is appointed first woman justice of the Supreme Court.

1983—U.S. troops invade island of Grenada.

1984—Reagan is reelected president. Democratic candidate Walter Mondale's running mate, Geraldine Ferraro, is the first woman selected for vice-president by a major U.S. political party.

1985—Soviet Communist Party secretary Konstantin Chernenko dies; Mikhail Gorbachev succeeds him. U.S. and Soviet officials discuss arms control in Geneva. Reagan and Gorbachev hold summit conference in Geneva. Racial tensions accelerate in South Africa.

1986—Space shuttle *Challenger* crashes shortly after takeoff; crew of seven dies. U.S. bombs bases in Libya. Corazon Aquino defeats Ferdinand Marcos in Philippine presidential election.

Index

Page numbers in boldface type indicate illustrations.

About the Author

Zachary Kent grew up in Little Falls, New Jersey, and received an English degree from St. Lawrence University. Following college he worked at a New York City literary agency for two years and then launched his writing career. To support himself while writing, he has worked as a taxi driver, a shipping clerk, and a house painter. Mr. Kent has had a lifelong interest in American history. Studying the U.S. presidents was his childhood hobby. His collection of presidential items includes books, pictures, and games, as well as several autographed letters.